GAUDENT ANGELI

Mary O'Malley was born in Connemara in Ireland and educated at University College Galway. She lived in Lisbon for eight years and taught at Universidade Nova. She served on the council of Poetry Ireland and was on the Committee of the Cúirt International Poetry Festival for eight years. She was the author of its educational programme. She taught on the MA programmes for Writing and Education in the Arts at NUIGalway for ten years, held the Chair of Irish Studies at Villanova University in 2013, and has held Residencies in Paris, Tarragona, New York, NUI Galway, as well as in Derry, Belfast. She is active in environmental education, specifically marine. She is a member of Aosdána and has won a number of awards for her poetry, including the 2016 Arts Council University of Limerick Writer's Fellowship. She is the Trinity Writer Fellow at the Oscar Wilde Centre for 2019. She writes and broadcasts for RTÉ Radio regularly.

GAUDENT ANGELI

MARY O'MALLEY

CARCANET

Acknowledgements

Thanks to the Glucksmann Library at the University of Limerick for commissioning 'In Athena's House' as one half of a double sonnet. Thanks to the Arts Council of Ireland and to the Oscar Wilde Writing Centre at Trinity College Dublin. A number of the poems in this book have appeared in *The Irish Times*, including 'In Athena's House'. 'An Easter Sonnett' was published as 'A Sonnet for Paris'. Other publications include *The Ogham Stone* and *PN Review*. A number of poems have been broadcast on RTÉ 1 and Lyric FM.

First published in Great Britain in 2019 by
Carcanet
Alliance House, 30 Cross Street
Manchester M2 7AQ
www.carcanet.co.uk

A CIP catalogue record for this book is
available from the British Library.
ISBN 978 1 78410 795 6

Book design by Andrew Latimer
Printed in Great Britain by SRP Ltd, Exeter, Devon

The publisher acknowledges financial
assistance from Arts Council England.

Supported using public funding by
ARTS COUNCIL
ENGLAND

CONTENTS

For Ethan and Nia

I

At the round earth's imagined corners, blow
Your trumpets, angels, and arise, arise
From death, you numberless infinities
Of souls, and to your scattered bodies go...
JOHN DONNE

MAKING MARMALADE
for Ethan

It's years since I've done it, this desperate stay
against mid-winter. Too much bother, headwreck
fuss, too many easier ways to spend time.
Now here they are, a hill of bitter oranges to climb.

A burst of solar flares; slice and chop, juice as sour
as hissop; it takes time to trap this in a jar.
The sharp blade, the pith and pit and slide of it,
the careful weighing of sugar. I stirred the pot

until the mess thickened and sweetened January.
All day I watched you watching the oranges circling
in their own solar system, orbiting the kitchen
in a slow whirl and – *Gaudent angeli!* –

kept there by love's uplifting force,
bright suns that spun around your absent face.

MAPPING

I am looking for the cobbler
who sewed up the bag of winds.
This is why I follow Odysseus
on his wanderings.

ONCE

It was the roustabout whirl
of the Siege-of-Ennis on the marquee floor
the hot night summer carnival
the fights, to-be-continued New Year

Easter, St Patrick's night, young men
letting off steam with fists, knives, the *scian*
the cut-and-come-again
flash of something dangerous, Borges' *vaiven*

flashing in the light of the disco ball. Women
screamed, one fainted in the direction
of the knifeman. Up on their tricks.
The lads ignored them, upped and skipped

to England, stayed gone until summer.
What she remembers is the last dance she got
the night it ended – a slow foxtrot,
how the band never stopped, just played louder.

Once it was all this and weekly confession.
The perils of translation –
the tramelled mind mistaking natural for wild –
now, it's a tourist slogan.

DUEL

A man in the garden with a sword danced,
just him and his invisible opponent,

a man, or it might have been a woman
so seductively he moved, or a friend

he stalked and would kill, no doubt
of that from the sudden slice across

the apple tree. Then I thought no,
he is fencing with his own shadow

and this is a fight to the death.
When I woke I heard a long breath

light as a moth at the window,
his parting bragadaccio.

IN THE NEW ROOM

Summer is dispelled by a few breaths
from the North. This room is the size
of the forge where a mare
allowed her bent leg to be placed
on the smith's knee, the old shoes
to be prised loose, the hooves trimmed
and a new set fitted. Silvery stamps.
I took it in, standing silent and thin
outside the door that rolled open
to metal, fire, horses and the men
mindful of their manners, the child
careful not to outstay her welcome.

This first morning standing
among the dead Greeks
nothing reaches me. This is how we are
when we go to war. The stove
is a bellows. The dark interior
fizzes with the hiss and bluster
of metal, the cluster of atoms
cooling at the join form a scar
as if an iron wheel is being forged,
when what I want is a poem open as a gold ring,
full of sky and a tree, copper-leaved,
such as tumbling coins are spun from.

It is time to praise what is broken,
the cracked bowl painted with a fish
in copper and clay, in one piece after six
hundred years of wars and carelessness.

Praise the countries that are torn North
from South, East from West.
Praise the houses that are ordinary,
not well built. Many do not have them.

That is your job, to praise the stricken,
the refugee girls drowned like kittens
and we've all seen the pictures
from bombed cities. Praise them.

It is easy to love the rose,
the whole man, the beautiful Maserati.
Dreaming of druids and ruins
has its compensations surely

but take this world rotten and venomous.
Praise it because it is yours.

MAYOR

after Amichai

It is hard to be the Mayor of Tribet.
How can you do anything with it
when people sleep on the street like dogs
and even respectable youngsters take drugs.

You clear the square of drunks and trees.
In the University there are endless rows
about money. Rocks fall onto cars.
Houses conspire to behave like slums.

Weeds blown in from the badlands root,
they flourish under the November moon.
The needles along the canal banks sprout.
Luckily the river carries our secrets out to sea.

Otherwise you could find anything in it –
bicycles, shopping baskets full of money,
nod-and-wink bag weighted with stone.
It's hard to keep it clean for the tourists.

Dogs sniff at the drugs on the river bank.
We have a culture business to run but people
sleeping in doorways are no help at all.
What can you do with a town like that?

SPELL

Tweet tweet. Sometimes the pecking sound
is all there is, sometimes the meme.
In the meaning, sometimes the warning.
Me me me me, me me meme. *Hey little darling*
tweet tweet tweet. The world is fifteen
much crossed, less kissed. *Hey little sweetheart*
hate hate hate sings the man in the machine.

The grown-ups, locked in their semis
in Gleann na mBodhar, immune
to the shrieks of the magical wars
in thrall to the piper so slick, slick, slick
singing *Hey little sweetheart, click, click, click*
stand at their windows, shining in the rain
waving Hamelin's children down the drain.

Said the Queen to Pope Benedict, 'How d'you do?
Our relations are Germans too.'
Said the Pope 'After you.'
She replied 'Take a pew.'
And they rested their rears
under fine chandeliers
and took tea and some sandwiches too.

Then they talked about weather,
the pagans and whether
his Christians or hers were for better or worse
nearly finished, and what could they do?
'Mine are costing a packet.'
'Mine are making a racket.'
'Between peasants and priests
one's family and tax
it's a struggle to know what to do.'

THREE TRIADS FOR ETHAN'S COMMUNION

I

Three gifts for you today:
Grace in the shining host
Joy in the high ball's arc
Freedom in the sea's wide reach.

II

May you always have:
Thrushes to circle your shining head
Hands to house your moth self
Music for the road heavenwards.

III

Three things for you to treasure:
The strands around Ireland
The thoughts in your mind
All the stories in the whole big world.

AT ELEVEN

To keep you safe in your boat
shakily moving away
little by little to fish
and try yourself out
is my birthday wish.

I know your course
has been set without us.
All I can do
is put this small compass
with hope
in a box for you.

A CHAIN

A girl outside a dark forge.
Inside, a white horse.
The glint of his new minted shoes.
The steady ring of the smith's hammer
linking them them together.

ON NIA'S BIRTHDAY

Two doves on the rooftop, one white
one grey, both hidden in plain sight.
One for the sun, one for the moon –
which are you, day or night?

GRAND NATIONAL

They met and married. They got
children. They loved one another
or didn't. He never meant
to be silent or frighten her.

She didn't set out to woo the child
over him but she won and there they lie,
chained to the nation's story, tired
race horses in their stalls.

Saint Mammy and Demon Daddy
with her rights, his wrongs.
Once or twice it's the other way round
but this is the nation's story, not theirs

the plot handed down *o glun go gluin*
from generation to generation.
The nation doesn't take kindly
to foreign interpretations

so round and round they go
in this story where the man and the woman
inherit their children's failings
and pass them on.

FAME

Suddenly without knowing, there is a change of course.
One minute you are writing stories of spare detail, to impress.

They love your distance, your safe hands, your cool intelligence.
Then the current shifts. You're out, it's time for passion

or they want the well turned couplet, neat as a Duchess's ankle.
Remember when you were everyone's darling ingénue?

They wanted you everywhere, like Aphrodite. You were exhausted.
Now you have silence. They claim to think you live abroad.

You can sing, burn time down to the last delicious drop,
let the wind play you, until it blows you out.

THREE THINGS

Today there are only three things:
oranges, a bridge, a river.

The oranges orbit the face of a juggler
who smiles in his halo of suns.

The bridge is a solid stone ship.
It connects the city to the island.

The river is the same one that slips
past the end of a garden

where the willows and the house stand
patient, expectant, silent.

The willow is waiting for leaves,
the house for love but today

there are only three things:
oranges, a river and a bridge.

DARK PRESENCE
for Patrick Graham

What embodies the dark presence
now that the gods have gone,
those gods that asked for a girl's life
asked her father to stick in the knife
in return for a fair wind, which he did.
A fair wind is not to be sniffed at
if you're a sailing man in search of revenge
but the same gods got children
on their daughters and played hell with
little red Gerion. As for the sons,
mostly pretty screwd up, as you'd expect.

They're gone. We're left to our own devices.
In what mask or state does their dark presence sit?
Is it in the river, the needle, the knife
in the manicured hands of the moneyman's wife
in the nooks and the crooks of the dark web?
Who, at the end, will turn out the lights?
And isn't it odd, that we miss them so much.

It is coming like zinc
the light hard as ice
on a bucket
injures the eyes. It cuts sideways
like knives, Gilgamesh
like acid thrown
in your face.

It is twenty seventeen
and something ugly is gathering
in the backstreets of the webworld,
in the fields, in the kitchens,
in the sewers
that funnel under facebook
and twitter and instagram
by the bright silvery light
of the moon.

The drones shovelling
their lives into pick-up trucks
blame it on the Mexicans,
the Irish, the blacks.
It is hard to be friendly
in this unfriendly time.
The puppet-masters are smiling
behind their endangered animal masks,
otter, lemur, baby bear.

IRONY

We didn't expect them back so soon –
the idols, with the gods leaving brusquely.
It seemed, we expected a new dawn
Or a cool intelligence to rule. We forgot
about hunger and want, that men
love war and blood sacrifice. Then
the idols came. The first ones were gold,
large and some said false, and vulgar.
Of course, they rusted.

Then salt. So small, we all got one.
Soon the new barbarians will come
and use them to flavour their stews.
They have their own gods, omniscient
just like the old ones. They will look inside
your dried-up soul and count your sins,
which they'll publish on the web.

THE IDOLS

The new gods live in Silicon Valley.
They play the world like mad children.
They too have pacts to keep.
They will meet their Nemesis
some ordinary day, over a smoothie
or a vegan fry. She will catch them gazing
into their own images and freeze the frame.
She will saunter over from behind the counter.
She's already on her way.

RIDDLE

Who laid the world egg?
Who will hatch it?
Who made this crazy dish?
Who will eat it?

INTERSECTING GROUND

According to Lao Tsu, whose book on war
was known among the poets,
there are nine grounds for the warrior
and only one appeals to me, the fifth.

I recognise it instantly, a high island
tethered lightly to location
where refugees and travellers land
and when they are refreshed, move on.

I read further and find this is the battlefield
which the warrior chooses
as his highest ground, a launching pad
for a young lord or duchess

with territorial ambition. I never knew till now
how many learned from old Lao Tsu.
I was taken up with living, and thought, like Prospero
my library was dukedom large enough.

AN EASTER SONNET

This is beauty, arms open, reaching upwards.
At first the mind refuses it, but the fire
is ravenous. It will have its sacrifice and does.
While it rages, the gold icon shimmers in kitchens,
on street corners, in bars from there to China.
The windows, the wash of light. Day in
day out. Memory refuses it.

Let reason sleep with reason's monsters.
This is Her day, Our Lady of Paris.
In the dead of night, the ruin shivers.
Its gargoyles climb down.
Statues in elegant robes roll up their sleeves.
The flying buttresses put their shoulders
to the wheel. It burns. It rises.

SAMHAIN AT CRÚACHAN AÍ

There's a time of year the annals reckon
when the veil between time and the worlds
is thin and pervious to two-way traffic.

It fell to Nera, a minor prince, to go out
and put a wicker anklet on a hanged corpse
on All Soul's Night to ward off disaster.

He was kidnapped by the dead and kept half a year,
forced to carry the hanged man
and other such tasks then considered

if not common, not outside reason.
When he came back through visions of a burning fort
and his people slaughtered,

with a bunch of summer flowers as proof
of his warnings, only an hour had passed
and the warriors were still dancing.

MY FIRST DEATH

It's all so long ago.
At the end of my first death
I found myself facing him
across a river. Just standing there
large as life, waiting.

He took my hand, led me
to a room, a table, a bed.
After five days, he let me go
with new life stirring in my blood,
handcuffed to his stars.

I went home. To start again, tidy up
the house, wash the dishes.
I put away the crystal, the good knives
put all in order, but someone
placed a bomb in our lives.

Pieces of ice lodged in us. That's how I died
the first time and woke up on the run
stroking a river. One star, the red one,
still there and the city,
full of humans like us in far orbits

cold as Mars, but visible,
close enough to hit against
accidentally and to hear
their voices in the fog. So long ago
my first death. So stealthy.

Then the nights were mine
until I died again.

THE HEART MAN

It is somewhere to the left
of centre. When he is asked
to picture it, he sees a dark space

a metal wrapping locked tight
to protect it from the touch of ravens
and whatever else is in there.

A shaman wants to flood it
with love, the healing breath,
lay all that raw flesh exposed

to his inner eye, pulsing red light.
The shaman tries and the casing creaks
in the man's chest. He is tired.

Next day, he wakes, decided.
'I will find my heart,' he says,
'and breathe on it

like an injured bird now that I know
where it is. I'll clean out the rust
myself and see what happens next.'

When he got it tuned he went to the pub
twice a week to hear music
that lifts the heart and makes time fly.

He was dancing with Madame Bonaparte
when it cut out. He folded so quietly that
the music played on, nice and stately.

DOMESTIC ADVICE

If you follow Scáthach or Macha,
women of distinction and war, and stir
what they give you into the pot,
expect to bring the house down
on everyone's head, including your own.

SAY YOU DIED

Say you died and there he was, God.
What would he look like now? A man.
What use is a goddess at times like this
with her knowing look, her
'Roll up your sleeves and get on with it'
or worse 'Because-you're-worth-it'
and a fridge full of lipstick.
Say he was old, with kind eyes and a beard.

Say you caught sight of yourself in the mirror
sitting in some outhouse in the afterlife
with boxes of lamps and tools for hoeing stars
and saw a child far from you, and walked up
to this tired God and lay your head on his knee and slept
as if it were your last sleep and your best.

TIME LAPSE
i.m. Steve McDonagh

November and I had been thinking of my dead
as I do every year, leafing through
their missed faces but you were never among them
though it has been long enough.

This morning, sending an email I type in 's'
and your name comes up at hotmail.com,
so real I want to write to you about this library
in the University in Barcelona,

ask what you think of independence for Catalunya
and our own celebrations and revisions of 1916,
cultural amnesia, milk of magnesia you'd say.
So this is where the emails stop

some ghost post office box in heaven
or purgatorio, Dante cycling his way through,
collecting evidence at dead letter drops.
Among these bookshelves in this lovely city

I see your house in Kerry, its China roses,
and miss our disagreements on the phone.
I'm glad of our last drive from Shannon
when you picked me up from a trip to Paris

and talked about your daughter and Artaud,
a lift I almost didn't take thinking
there would be other times and swimming at Menard.
But friends die, and so do conversations.

I don't know why you waited until now
to join the dead, or I to say goodbye.

SONG I

He'll come when he's ready
not a second before his time
welcome him or fight with him
but don't invite him in.
When you feel his shadow
smoothing down your hair
step out onto the doorstep
and wait to greet him there.
With his greengold eyes
and his voice so rare
with his scythe and his scissors
and his needle full of air.

IN THE LIGHTHOUSE TOWER

The mindhorse splinters and bucks. It pitches
down the twelve-foot waves, and slides
into the trough, eyes rolling, mane
askew, legs kicking for purchase at a slant
too oblique for comfort until the wave recedes
and the shore rights itself. Remount.

This is no one-day storm.
Choked by grief without grief's solace
that what is lost might be found
the mind locks down in its own hell
with unspeakable things scurrying in corners.

Then the soul moves out over the yard
to the old house, across the plain of Moytura,
passes the grave of Noah's daughter
travels to a cave under a hill on the coast
and brings back salt, fresh air, an anchor.

But we are forbidden the soul – hollow words
have replaced it. The age is splintered.
We have not found the forged conscious easy
nor forging it, been thanked.
The mindhorse settles into a steady trot.

In the cold light that reaches deep
just off the edge where the cliff ends unmapped
the fingers slip and time uncoils,
a gutter of fallen leaves. Europe
is coming unstitched again. We call on hope.
She may not come.

Time for the new, a breakthrough
from elsewhere, a rocket escape
to a frozen rock, frontiers razored
in the ice of space – the gyre spinning slowly
through it all. Each age has its letter
given or made, M, the thirteenth.

The grown child, the mother, even the fry
with their eight steadying fins
have a quark on the great wheel
which moves through the dark side
past the lighthouse, over the shore

down our road and on into the sun,
neither caring nor uncaring endlessly,
but marked and transformed by each other
as quarks are, then it spins great bolts
of electricity or love, and holds us steady.

So we sing ourselves on because of joy
or when there is none, because we must.

A JIG IN SPACETIME
i.m. Alec Finn

At half past four on Wednesday afternoon
instead of working I went by invitation
to a quiet pub in Oranmore where I learned

that Mont Cisco is in Corofin
to avoid soundmen in leather trousers,
that the greyhound at the bar drinks gin

while the horse beside her is a Guinness man
and objects to talking dogs and bodhrans,
that a wild duck can lead a hawk astray.

Then the fiddles, the bazouki and the box kicked in.
They led us to to 'The Sean a Mhac Tube Station'
one of seven stops on the Cosmic Line

a wormhole in spacetime built by navvy musicians
where they tunnelled and played to bring here there
and there here, where the pieces of a broken cup

could fly back up and reassemble in the hand, time
after sweetened time, Mr Feynman
until the tunes stopped and the train reversed.

BLACK SWAN

There's a woman with a broken knee
who keeps taking taxis to Nowhere
in search of the driver who swims at night
because, he once told her he likes
to hang out with the fish in the dark
and look in at the lights in Claddagh.
In his wetsuit he might be a black swan.

She's read about Schemkel, the stammering angel
god kicked out for letting sinners
into heaven without a visa. It might be him
living in Galway in direct provision.
She wants to know his name in case
he is that shy angel, an unlikely fruit
fallen into her pandemonium.

THE TRAMPS

Fish shoal, birds flock, sheep mostly follow.
Their herd sense is old. The tiger, the wolf, the fox
and the odd expelled runt make their own way.
On a hill outside the city, the scapegoat stands.
She cries at night, foraging on the city dump.

She searches in the rubbish mounds for bones.
Sometimes she sees stars sharp as diamonds
reflected in a pool of filth. When she finds
a high-heeled shoe, sequinned and the right fit
she sees a girl in a red dress, the men watching
saying 'Perfect for a wedding', how they lean
forward in the limelight, then she drives hersef on
arrayed in rags, old mobile phones and pearls.

Her dreams are spiked with bits of coloured glass
and the odd sapphire. Nights are the worst
but lately she has found others like herself
sent out with suitcases full of the town's sins.
They form their own small tribe. They talk often
about how, soon now, they will lay the baggage down
and walk away, empty of past and future.

THE ISLAND

The islanders, spotting a ship passing Brightcity
lit and full of dancing healthy couples from the past
get sick suddenly with strange diseases
common to foreign parts – Ebola and the like.

The ship sails on into the past. It will dock
in Brazilia ten minutes before it left port.
On the island, there is fighting, hunger,
trouble with women but their hearts aren't in it.

A stranger arrives with a stick he claims
is the the staff of Christ. A madman.
They stop fighting long enough to send him
to the mainland in manacles to be locked up.

They pitied Antonin Artaud. They understood
his sickness, natural in the circumstances.

MOTH LIFE

Cleaning behind the sofa I came across one
on the floor, a dessicated husk, its tiny sails
inscribed with 'om ' or 'pi', or some pale
encrypted code written by owls.

Space is full of them, ghost moths
beating towards our light, particles
made manifest, the patterned wings'
fine brushstrokes figuring matter

as they fly, silent as child ghosts
their poems emit silver pulses,
mysterious and steady
as Rimbaud's illuminations.

CALENO CUSTURE ME

What were you doing, a chailín óg
astray among the maids and trollops
stripped of your diphthongs
so far from home with a war on.

Some say our tricky language
found purchase in the Bard's pen.
You were just a stream of gibberish
canonical babble on a fool's tongue.

Whether you are the girl
from the banks of the River Suir
or the love of his heart
you slipped into history by the back door

floated in on the line, a lark
in London, light as a breath of fresh air
among the servants and kings
and the 'what ish my nation' talk.

Agus Cailín Óg, a stór
you are still there.

ATLANTICA

You get tired of being wild.
The crest torn from a wave in wind
is an everyday thing, the peregrine
on his rock wants to go back
to normal life, before he was feral
or endangered or a raptor.
Maybe he liked being just a hawk.

You want to go out in your boat and fish
without bailiffs arriving to board
as if they were the U.S. navy
and you were hiding a catch
of immigrants for the black market.
Making you put out your cigarette.

You want to be on the strand in the sun
watching the purplish shifts in a pool
at lowtide and not feel ashamed
to know every inch of shore
but not the proper names for things,
nor all the scientific implications.

You know enough. You have to listen
to thunder, but even the indifferent sea
gets tired of everything being marvellous.
It is choking on plastic adjectives
and an insulted sea rises.
You know what that means.

NEWS

He knows by the horses
that are everywhere in the fields

unemployed, their gaze
fluent as verses,

put aside for years
with the rosary beads and prayers

but lately plentiful again
as primroses or furze;

by the quick shivers of their skin
he knows they are listening

to news that concerns
our fate and theirs.

'The clear pure Heaven yearns to wound the earth
and yearning seizes the Earth to wed the Heavens –
rain comes down from the throbbing skies
and pierces the Earth, she teems with flocks
and Demeter's full rich life that strengthens men,
and from the drenching marriage rite the woods,
the spring bursts forth in bloom. And I, I cause it all.'

AESCHYLUS

'And if the soul
is to know itself
it must look into a soul:
the stranger and enemy, we've seen him in the mirror.'

GEORGE SEFERIS, *'Mythistorema'*

HORSE

The black horse stood on the shore.
He pawed the ground, galloped down
to the high-water mark, let out
syncopated snorts. He roared

'This is my island. Who are you?'
His front hooves looked dangerous.
I jumped up and slapped his puss
with my gloves. Three times. 'Whoah!

I only speak to white horses. Where
are the friendly mares
that understand my dreams?'
'Gone, he said. I am the only islander.'

No more the flesh-eating mares of Diomedes –
Terrible, Shining, Swift, Yellow Skin.
They were my friends.
'Make do with what's sent or make nothing.

My name is Arion, Demeter's rape-child
not that accompanist you were in thrall to
with his dithyramb dirumbs.'
I turned to go. 'Get up on my back.

I'll carry you.' He knelt. I mounted.
We went. I climbed down, tired.
He cantered back into the tide.
Something out-of-kilter, a skipped drumbeat

in his stride made me look round.
Then I recognised him by his human feet.

DEMETER'S SEARCH

My evening star is hollow
and the moon a flat drum
that does nothing for me now
after years bleeding me dry.

My morning star is down
and won't show herself.
She is buried underground
where no signals reach her.

Nothing will grow anywhere
until I find her – no flowers
no crops and the years
will have no flavour.

HOUSE

It stands upright with an air
not of abandonment exactly
more of a woman
waiting for her daughter
to come through the gate, a mother
flayed of expectation.
It is losing heart.

This does not show except
in unguarded moments,
evenings when it sags
inwards, its many eyes
darkened with rain.
The roof slumps over the eaves
like tired hair.

The house wants so little,
the squeak of a gate opening,
the girl's face
shining on the path.
Let me tell you something
about houses, they too
are spancelled to the past.

ROOM

I can see your hair on the pillow
a cat's marmalade face beside your own
'I snuck Fa Fa in'
black and orange under the moon.
Useless to ask how
the thread snapped or who will repair
such a delicate thing, or when
the dark shiver of your roots
will uncoil in whatever night
holds it there. Only the light
knows the light's path through
the spiralling stream of your hair
and the woman with the needle and thread
sitting invisibly there by your bed.

SILENCE

Send something – a pink leather boot
the fairy money from your first milk tooth
Matilda signed by Roald Dahl in Kennys
a pig emptied of silver and pennies.

Send the hairy bow from your small violin
the velvet dress scattered with sequins
just like the one in Las Meninas.
Send a look, an answer, a small bird
until something melts and you send word.

DESCENT

I have looked for you among the Greeks
where hate and love are close as blood
and blood is worth so much and no more

I went down among the Greeks reluctantly
not trusting in cheap plunder but there is
no more time. Threads have been pulled

time woven, knotted, snipped. I went
to the cities and the far islands
and met statues, women with blind eyes

and no mercy. In temples and bars and houses
everywhere I saw your likeness, and everywhere
women with their bored gaze

fixed beyond me, on some blue island
with dolphins, an olive tree, the dangerous bull
in his maze, and the woman who holds the thread.

None of them spoke to me, just one more
crazed mother searching for her daughter.
They're used to that there.

VIGIL

I have paid the coin time has extracted
with another in my mouth for the shroud
a willing deposit for when you are found.

I will stand in the helical stream with the winds
scorching my ankles until someone looks up
and says 'Bargain'. Then I will go down

to meet her and bring the small red
seeds of the sun to remind her of home.
I will stand there until the dark breaks open.

MASK

She closes the front door
and steps into the car –
cold, hieratic, nubian.
Her face shut tight is hard
and beautiful. Pain
has sludged in charred
circles under her eyes.
Words crack like ice.
Some snake has sucked
the sweetness from her voice
and the joy from her lovely face.

QUESTION

When you have gone so low
that you would bend down and pull
grass with your bare fingers, bow
your head into the winter muck to dull
what cannot be borne, surely it is time
to look up from the ruins of this future
and ask were they in on this
from the start, the Weird Sisters?

Were they sitting on your cradle
pitching curses down the female line
like frogs, switches that would flick on
and deliver shots of wasp venom
with the three-in-one inoculation;
and if they were, where is the godmother
with the antidote to rhyme a cure
and weave out of smashed glass
and torn dresses, a bridge of sorts
that you could walk across
to reach your daughter above the fester
and fog with hyacinths and roses.

GIFT

This morning I woke with ease
because Persephone was back with me
smiling and talking as it used to be.
I felt no pain and my skin was young.
I was happy in the dream's wash
all day. That was peace
the gift of a time folding away.

MYTH

What we have of them is hearsay
some pictures on vases,
a mosaic that could have been anyone
and the stories, more or less alike

go like this: a young woman
was gathering flowers when the ground
opened and a man took her, a god.
The story is about Demeter's grief

so great it parched the earth
shrivelled crops, stopped all growth
that brought the gods to the table.
The story is about a mother's love.

A young girl is eating poemegranates,
their little seeds between her teeth.
One stuck. Should she have fasted?
For that slip up she got six months

year in, year out. Her mother got life
watching her emerging from the dark,
eyes hurting, the light
x-raying her bones. Soon the girl asked

for a wrap of shadow around her. Why?
All we have are fragments, rumours.
We pick among them for a key to unlock
the hieratic text of our lives. Over and over.

HISTORY

This story is about a mother and a daughter,
a god taking what he wanted, Demeter's girl.
All we know of them is hearsay, some figures
on vases, the woman with her sheaf of corn.

Her rage stopped the harvest.
Bare shelves brought the gods to the table.
This story is about a bargain, and a trick,
a young girl eating a pomegranate

A seed in her teeth. The girl has no say
in our best-known versions. We see her
climbing from the dark, eyes hurting,
the light x-raying her bones. Year in, year out.

Demeter might have said 'Stay if it's easier.
Let the crops rot', but the myth needed growth.
This is no time for shady business, the bargains
and chains. We too live in important places.

Let the books remember the local battles.
Re-write the plot. Let the harvest wither.
This is your life. She is your great event.
Keep her in the sun.

MIRROR MIRROR

I

There's a looking glass at the end of the hall
full of the frozen smiles
and coloured lenses of cut out eyes.

Faces swim in its depths, shapes
dim as old memories.
I have looked into its shallows for a long time.
It will remember my face.

II

It's not much of a life since I moved in.
My loved ones are there but I can't touch them.
When they see me looking most
swim slowly back into the depths
but sometimes one rises to the surface
as if longing for a kiss.

LITTLE DAZZLER

There are limits to the thing itself.
Too many condoms, smartphones, blood

can turn into blocks of wood
everyday words playing dead.

Take that snowdrop, the white head
bent among a tangle of dead thyme,

a supermodel in a green tube dress.
Odysseus's charm against the sorceress

should be yesterday's news,
but Holy Moly she still dazzles.

III

THE BEE AND THE HELICOPTER

Before I knew about time
when they talked about the dead
drumming and dancing in the air
I believed them.

Could it be you positioned the bee
with his hexagon stare
when it locked into mine
in mid-air on my walk to the point,

when the sky thrummed with a beat
that held us there – the bee, the stone tower,
yourself both here and there or neither
like Schrodinger's cat-in-the-box.

A dot in the sky and a helicopter
the size of a wasp, of a merlin,
of those painted angels that hold up
the earth's corners, came into her own.

Then she flew on. Before I knew about time,
how it curves back, how it could be a sea
we sail on, that perhaps
when that woman sat at our births

doling out thread, the skein was the myth
and it was this world her sister would snip
with the shears at the end, snatching us up,
dropping us down in some alien place.

The night that Californian came to dinner
uninvited and gave a sermon
against smoking, ranting like a Missioner
when Jamie said 'Come on, I need a fag after that' –

the fun we had afterwards, do you remember?
No theory of time can bring me your voice
the whole low laugh of you here now
catching up on gossip, on years, on great slices

of our one precious life, missed.
Sometimes you are near and the air fills
with dancing and marching and things
we could bear there and we cannot bear here.

That's when I tell myself stories – that it was you.
The bee and the stone tower were your signals
that the helicopter angel was circling back,
and I would believe them

but for the evening sun, the engine's rhythm
chopping the air, cutting out squares of time,
nailing them down, moving on out. There is no echo
from your silence but the call of a curlew.

THE PENTAQUARK

Looks like a cross between
the Holy Ghost and a dragonfly.
It has wings at the end of its heel
and it stings. It is notoriously shy.

It has a big job in the Universe,
something vital like holding up Venus.
It's the new kid on the block
and they say we'd be nowhere

without it. The Pentaquark.
How about that now, Mr Mark?

TIME TRAVEL

We'd all like to fly
by our co-ordinates
live in them alone
just a shiny-breasted equation
without the front door
gables, geometry
of roof to solid wall
but we have flesh to feed,
skin for the sea-swim
and the glorious hope
of a few more cuckoos.

After that, maybe to live on
without all this flesh and bother
is not as preposterous
as economics, endless war,
Or twitter.

AT THIS LATE STAGE THE GYPSY SAID

I'm going to stake it all on hope
a craft as safe as any other
the last trick in the box
brighter than most and ditch
the old stays and corsets worn
too long against despair
around the heart and never worked.
It's as raw now
as at the hour of birth.

I want to taste the red juice
of pomegranate – the seeds
like babies' teeth
all the sweeter for being brief –
and tell the time by water-clock.
Granada is the place
for me. Who knows?
On the long way round by sea
I might meet a dolphin
or a sunfish, or a salmon going home.

Then inland through the bitter hills
where villages perch like brides
waiting to be snatched by boys
on vertiginous motorbikes
and deflowered willingly in caves.
I will keep going and where I can, sing
until I reach the Albaicin
and rest and listen to the water
laughing in cisterns, and dream.

SPACE. TIME. CURVE

He was my knife then.
There were flashes
of steel in the sun.
He cut an orange into quarters
and handed me one,
the blade sweet with juice.

That's how it was in the sun,
strawberries for lunch and a swim
into life itself. Life tastes
of salt and strawberries
and the flat lick of steel
then the sting of a thorn in your heel

when time swerves and curls
backwards and we're poised
at the top of a wave all unfurled
the girl, the fruit and the man
with the knife in his hand.

GYPSY POEM II

When I was young
I gave my heart to him
to put beside his own and keep it.
As well to have laid it in a basket
of lobsters for protection.
I've got it back at last, bruised,
unwrapped and worse for wear
but beating, pushing it's planets
and tide through my veins
surprising me with its firepower.

SOUL SISTER

So there you are again, Psyche
dolled up in your fur and finery
good legs, cheekbones like blades
looking like you've been to hell
and back and 'Let me tell you,
it was wonderful'. I'm glad one of us
had fun and still, in spite of provocation
stays much the same. Upbeat.

You've been banned, debunked,
banished. Why are you standing there
like that woman who drives a chariot
out across the stars – you're some man's
glorious nonsense – if not Plato's, whose?
For one attached to me at birth
you look as if you couldn't care less
but I missed you when you ditched me.

You don't get a person of your own
these days like a pet, you've become
a state of mind or something nebulous,
a fairy angel, kind and vacuous.
Go back, you're too much work.
You have that look, as if you'll never die.
Light me a candle in Notre Dame
and on a piece of paper they supply

for supplications write, *She wants to know*
where the spirit goes in winter.

BLOOD MOON

Under a spent volcanic cone the waves
still whisper and roar in the cave

where a woman who loved a drowned man
hid for a month until they found them.

The same lunatic moon shines now
as in nineteen thirty-nine,

the same virgin moon, her hymen
stitched in gold and silk. Men

with their crazed desire to be the first
have made her a wise old witch.

There is still blood, a lake of dark red
into which she dips her tired white head.

She hates wisdom when she remembers
the girls, their first clueless stirrings.

Such beauty, whole fields of daughters
their faces shining with laughter

and the horses ploughing at midnight
under cold famine light.

SONG II

Come cuckoo, come swallow
fold up the grey blanket
of winter and shake out
the new sheets
made out of triangles
sheared from the air.
Make me a summer
and fill it with esses
swimming over our heads
and your calls full of blue morning.

SWEENEY POEMS

I
Achill

She asked me, the woman, to watch out for the hawk.
He would slaughter her chickens, tear their gizzards
open, purses full of gravel. That speck high as the sun
cloaked like a prince is him. A squawk, hens scatter

as he swoops I remember – I was a prince.
I fill up. To be reduced to this, a scarecrow
when I would have had him on my fist, trained
dressed in my white robe with its embroidered gold.

I am a crippled thing, my mind poked by a child
with a stick. That's their gods for you. Sweeney cursed.
Look at my blue eyes. My world is injured. I'm a man
wracked on a new god's whim, not a broken bird.

II
Song of the Travelling Man

This morning language is collapsing
and exploding
like a volcano emptying.
Sparks are flying out of the words.
Words are crashing like meteorites,
lumps of dead iron in my mouth.
I can only say cold grey things.

At other times words cut, knives
true and sharp. They quiver
when their points hit home
blades in timber.
I watch them leave my mouth
a stream of tempered steel
and hear them whine past,
tall slim screams.

They turn to lumps of rust
every time and I regret them
but when it comes on again
I forget until the madness fades.
Then I remember and hide my face.

I'm a man, even then, even
when my mind turns on me
a wolf in a frenzy,
a hurt savage.

SWEENEY AWAY

This morning I went up the street where the dragons live.
They were spreadeagled on their balconies, copperwinged.
I wanted to go up to one of them and ask why they hung
over the street like bats and whose curse caused
them to roost like this, beautiful monsters suspended
over a balcony in Barcelona
but the fire was in me and I bounded on.

SWEENEY WATCHES AT A WINDOW

This morning you too are rising from sleep
swimming slowly up through dim shapes,
your darkfish, or down from the light regions
where a boy sits eating cake under the table,
his parents' voices 'aisy and slow', the pillars
of their legs akimbo, licking the cream from a slice
of last night's cake, safe for the last time.

Even bankers sleep and rise from their beds.
These November nights, with their moon
of bone, nobody's white sheet is seamless
in the morning. Especially not the boy
who was happy in his house under the table
nor his mother who wishes she had known
he was there, nor his father, who moved on.

THE DATE

It's never as you expect it to happen.
The woman, late on New Year's night
waits in the house on the Fontanka.
The one has not arrived
to whom she can offer Russia. She is alight
with her own suffering, a gilded icon
with a slash of red lipstick. She writes
in the air, on her tongue, on ice. She lights
candles, lays out crystal for wine.

She does this because a poet
does not give up when the expected
hero lets her down. She drinks alone
and sits on, working until dawn.
Of the hero, his missed chance
nothing is recorded but absence
burning like an icicle lamp.

A HEARTBREAKER

I know the lure of golden birds
but there is no Byzantium for me
he said, or words to that effect
because he would not lie, not at the end.
His life was stretching behind him
like the *Deutschland* wreck,
nuns drowned, the faith they stood for
spent in a riptide of madness.
Women were seduced, and driven away.
Time after cyclical time
he was driven from himself
when his mind went astray.

Lithium couldn't save him
from the Union dead, his statuary
ancestors demanding their say
but it let him have some peace.
His final say were poems
the literal-minded missed.
They trembled with light,
the sighs of his own shade
approaching in a New York cab.

IN THE WORDSHED

He woke at three in the morning to a book
like an old fashioned bill
presented in a thick plastic folder with a pen
and through the night the Greek lines
moving through Irish into English flowed
through his notebooks from a basement room
a chemistry of debt and vexations
a deck of cards stacked.

Of course, he said over his coffee and croissant,
I prefer Greeks at war to Ireland at peace
but I think, on the whole, I'll stick with the French
and dig up Echo's bones at a safe distance.

THE WILDCAT

His mind bucks and belts around
scatterbrain, scattergun. He is trained
to whip thoughts into line

marshal them into regiments
and frogmarch them to a conclusion.
Turn his back for a second

and they're off, a herd of wildcats
over the wall, through a gap, up a tree
where one sits washing her face

just out of reach. He waits quietly
and hears a soft rustle.
She crawls down into his lap.

He's never seen this one before.
Well, he thinks, look what we've got here.
When she opens her green eyes

and he dives into them. In a flash
it's all done and she's gone, her pattern
scored on his dimensions.

TRANSLATION

Odysseus sails out, century after century
and keeps returning, each time a little changed
so that you wonder if, even once, he meets himself
coming home, but must still go on endlessly
each time with small degrees of change, which have,
by the journey's end, vast consequences.

Each generation he leaves Penelope again
sleeps with other women, puts a burning stake
in the Cyclops' eye and shows no great hurry
to get home until the sea has had enough of him
and we have run out of words for the sea's disorder
for the detailed ways a man can slaughter.

Then a fresh-painted ship sails into view
and we're lured back out the sea roads, into the blue.

THE WOLF

There was nothing to hold
when the lonely dance
that ends in nakedness
was over. He crossed her road
some late animal limping home.
His eyes shone in the carlight,
eyes already gone.
A vixen coughed outside her den
in the cruel starlight.
She drove on.

IN ATHENA'S HOUSE

This house is domestic, safe for take-off.
Nooks, books, at the window the necessary wolf.

The mind opening meets his stare and worries
at its own thirst. A boy struts in, the man you'll marry.

The hunt begins. There are diversions. Heroes
with studs and tattoos that play to the audience.

The rasp of teeth on the back of your neck
reminds you of your purpose. It pulls you back.

Walls dissolve in the mind-altering spaces
among the quarks, quincunx and gobsmack,

new stars greet old angels between June pages,
and from the floor along the stacks

a low growl as you fall softly on a thought
briefly disturbs the silence. Your first rebel act.

GOLDFINCHES

Who can believe that God plays dice
and make a way through life?

A foot from the window a cloud
of goldfinches descend on the niger seed.

Nothing I have done merits this charm
their cat faces yellow and red, as if

exotic flowers had taken to the air
transformed and came here

to Seanbháile, Maigh Cuilinn, the world
our egocentric sun revolves around

as Shakespeare saw the sun spin
around the earth because we all cling

when all the Gods are banished down
to Saturn or Pandemonium

to a steady planet with a friendly sun
circling around us, even Einstein.